D1120050

Viva Mexico!

The Past

George Ancona

BENCHMARK **B**OOKS

MARSHALL CAVENDISH
NEW YORK

To Trini Barnes

Gracias to Biblioteca Nacional de
Antropología e Historia, Centro de
Estudios de Historia de Mexico
Condumex, Centro Nacional de las Artes,
Matthew J. Dudley of Candlepants, Inc.,
Fomento Cultural Banamex, A.C.,
Fototeca Nacional de I.N.A.H., The
Hispanic Society of America, Museo de
Intervenciones, Genoveva Lopez Rosales,
José Manuel Springer.

Benchmark Books
Marshall Cavendish Corporation
99 White Plains Road
Tarrytown, NY 10591-9001
Website: www.marshallcavendish.com
Copyright © 2002 by George Ancona

Library of Congress Cataloging-in-Publication Data
Ancona, George.
The past / by George Ancona.
p. cm. – (Viva Mexico!)
Includes index.
ISBN 0-7614-1330-8
1. Mexico—History—Juvenile literature. [1. Mexico—History.] I. Title. II. Series.
F1208.5 .A63 2001 972—dc21 00-068046

Printed in Hong Kong
6 5 4 3 2 1

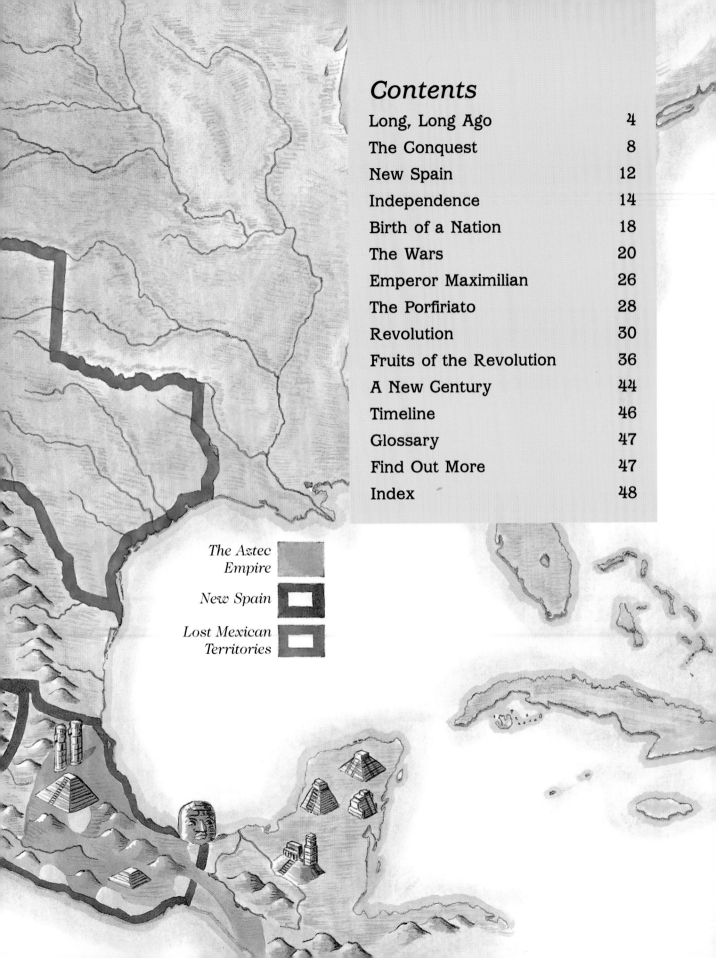

Contents

The Aztec Empire

New Spain

Lost Mexican Territories

Long, long ago

The story of Mexico begins long, long ago. Many different tribes once roamed the lands between North and South America. About nine thousand years ago they learned how to grow corn. The people settled down to farm, and communities and cultures were born.

About 1200 B.C., the Olmecs created a great civilization along the east coast of the lands called Mesoamerica. It lasted a thousand years. They built pyramids, temples, and ball courts and left behind giant heads carved in stone. In time, the Zapotecs of the southwest and the Maya of the southeast also built magnificent ceremonial centers.

The great city of Teotihuacán, which means the place of the gods, rose about 200 B.C. in the central valley of Mexico.

An Olmec head

An Olmec pyramid

The pyramid of the sun in Teotihuacán

Tezcatlipoca

By A.D. 650, the city was mysteriously abandoned. About 350 years later, a tribe from the north called the Toltecs, meaning "the artists," arrived in the valley of Mexico. Their gods were the plumed serpent Quetzalcoatl, god of creation and brotherhood, and Tezcatlipoca, god of night and the underworld. The arts, religion, and culture of the Toltecs were adopted by the other people of Mesoamerica.

Quetzalcoatl

5

Around 1250 a band of fierce warriors from a distant island called Aztlán, the place of the long legged birds, entered the Valley of Mexico. They called themselves the México, but today they are known as the Aztecs. A prophecy said they were to build a city at the place where they saw an eagle perched on a cactus eating a snake. When the Aztecs reached Lake Texcoco, they came upon the eagle. By 1325 they began to build the great city of Tenochtitlán on manmade islands. This is where Mexico City stands today.

The arrival of the México

The city of Tenochtitlán

The Aztecs built temples to worship Tlaloc, the rain god, and Huitzilopochtli, the god of war, whose symbol was the sun. In the temple of the sun stood a carved stone disk, sometimes called the Aztec calendar. In the center was the face of the sun god whose tongue represents the obsidian knife used to cut out the hearts of sacrificial victims. Their blood ensured that the life-giving sun would return each day. The Aztecs ruled an empire that lasted until the coming of the *conquistadores*, the Spanish conquerers.

The sun stone, sometimes called the Aztec calendar

7

The Conquest

On February 18, 1519, an adventurous conquistador, Hernán Cortés, sailed from Cuba with eleven ships carrying soldiers, horses, and cannons. When he reached the island of Cozumel off the coast of Yucatán, Cortés was welcomed by the Maya, one of the great cultures of Ancient Mexico. He also met a shipwrecked Spaniard, Jerónimo de Aguilar, a priest who had been with the Maya for seven years and learned their language. Aguilar happily joined Cortés's expedition.

The Spanish sailed north to the mainland. Hostile Maya attacked them but were soon defeated.

As peace offerings, the Maya gave the victorious Spanish gifts of gold and a young slave girl named Malinali, or, as she was later called, *La Malinche*. Cortés christened her doña Marina. She spoke her native Nahuatl, the Aztec language, and had learned Maya from her captors. Then the expedition continued north along the coast to the land of the Aztecs.

When the Aztecs heard of the newcomers, they thought Cortés was Quetzalcoatl, the fair skinned, bearded god who, according to legend, had sailed away on a raft of snakes promising to return. Unsure, the Aztec ruler Montezuma II sent messengers to greet the strangers. Doña Marina translated Nahuatl into Maya, which Aguilar then translated into Spanish for Cortés.

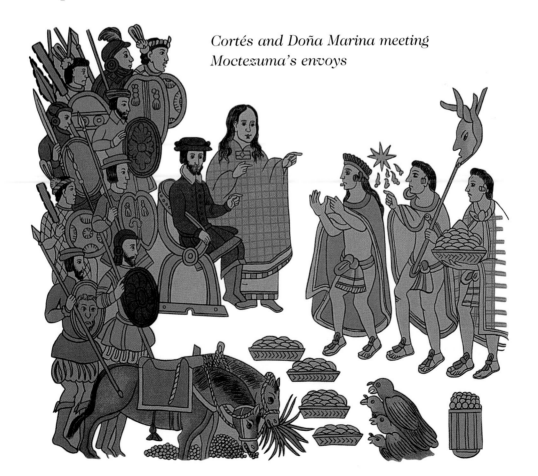

Cortés and Doña Marina meeting Moctezuma's envoys

Moctezuma greets Cortés.

When the Spanish army entered Tenochtitlán,
they were amazed by its size and beauty.
Montezuma II welcomed them with gifts of gold,
housed them in a palace, and offered them
chocolate to drink. The Aztecs soon found that
these men were not gods. The Spaniards captured
Montezuma and forced him to ask his people to
surrender. In anger, the Aztecs stoned their king to
death and decided to fight the invaders.

One night the outnumbered Spanish made their escape, but they lost many men. This was called *La Noche Triste*, the sad night, when Cortés cried for all the men he had lost. He fled to Tlaxcala, where he rested among his Indian allies and planned his return to Tenochtitlán.

In the beginning of 1521, Cortés returned to Lake Texcoco. His men built small boats with a cannon in each. Then the Spanish, along with their Indian allies, surrounded the city and attacked. The Aztecs fought bravely for three months until their leader Cuauhtémoc was killed. Cortés leveled the city and on the ruins built Mexico City, the first capital of New Spain. The conquistadors went on to defeat the vast empire of the Aztecs in four years.

This codex shows Moctezuma as a prisoner.

The Battle of Tenochtitlán. Cortés orders small boats built to attack the city.

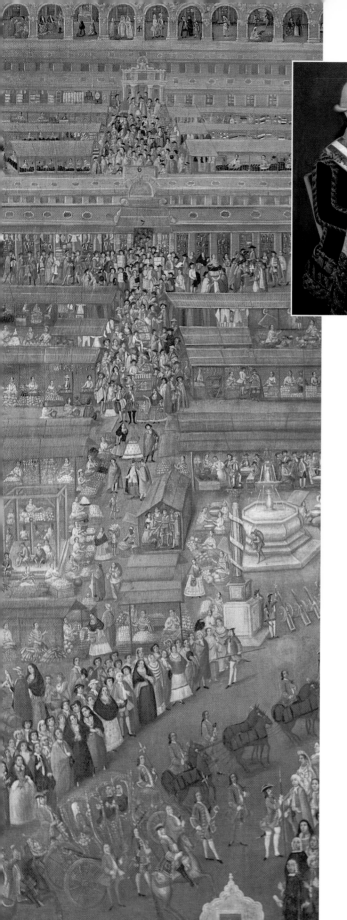

A viceroy

New Spain

The Spanish king sent a viceroy, or vice king, to govern the colony. The conquistadors were rewarded with land and Indian slaves. Many Indians died from European diseases and heavy labor. To replace them the Spanish brought in African slaves. A caste system ensured that the whites were privileged. Those who were born in Spain were called *peninsulares*. Those born in New Spain were called *criollos*. The children of white and Indian parents were called *mestizos*. Those of black and white parents were called *mulatos*. Indians were at the lowest level of the society.

A viceroy arrives in New Spain.

Indian slaves working for Spaniards

Catholic priests also came to New Spain to convert the Indians to Catholicism. They burned their codices, books of parchment that pictured their customs, religion, and science. They taught the Indians Spanish and European ways. The ancient temples were torn down, and the stones used to build churches. Church steeples soon rose above cities, towns, and villages.

Explorers claimed more and more land for New Spain, which became the largest Spanish colony in the world.

Church steeples rise over a Zapotec palace.

A detail of a mural showing Father Hidalgo's cry for social justice, which began Mexico's revolution

A statue of Hidalgo overlooks the bullet pocked granary.

Independence

By 1810, New Spain had been a colony for almost three hundred years. Many *criollos* were angry because a few rich Spaniards controlled the country. The rest of the people were terribly poor. Inspired by the French and American revolutions, a group of middle-class *criollos* gathered to plan an uprising against Spain. Among the rebels were Ignacio de Allende, a cavalry captain, and a priest named Miguel Hidalgo y Costilla.

On Sunday, September 16, 1810, in the town of Dolores, Father Hidalgo rang the church bells and gave the famous *grito*, the call for justice that sparked the revolution. Hidalgo led an army of 20,000 poor to the city of Guanajuato. They demanded that the mayor surrender. Instead, he and 200 of the king's soldiers and 150 Spaniards brought the city's treasury and barricaded themselves in a stone granary.

The rebels opened fire but were unable to break in. A young Indian miner nicknamed *El Pípila* (the turkey) strapped a flat stone on his back to shield him from the bullets. Holding a torch, he crawled like a turtle toward the granary and set fire to the wooden doors. The rebels charged through the charred doors and killed everyone inside. This was the first battle of the revolution, a war for Mexican independence that would last eleven long years.

The statue of El Pípila *overlooks Guanajuato.*

Father José María Morelos

The following year, in a battle with the king's royalist troops, Hidalgo and Allende were captured and executed. Their heads were cut off, put into cages, and hung from the corners of the granary at Guanajuato. José María Morelos, a *mulato* shepherd, mule handler, and priest became the new leader of the revolution. After many victories he too was captured and executed in 1815. General Vicente Guerrero, the son of black slaves, went on to lead the rebellion.

Searching for a way to resolve the conflict that had caused so much death and destruction, a

A detail of a mural showing General Vicente Guerrero

group of *criollos* asked the royalist colonel Agustín de Iturbide to meet with General Guerrero. In an unexpected turn of events, Iturbide decided to join the rebel cause for independence. Together he and Guerrero wrote the *Plan de Iguala* about how Mexico should be governed once it was independent.

Iturbide then led the rebel army to victory, and on September 21, 1821, they marched into Mexico City. The last viceroy, Juan O'Donohú, a Spanish liberal of Irish descent, recognized the people's call for independence, and so the nation of Mexico was born.

General Iturbide and the victorious insurgents enter Mexico City.

Coronation of the Emperor Agustín I

Birth of a Nation

Many people fought over what kind of
government to have. General Iturbide
formed a congress that agreed that
Mexico should be an empire. On May 19,
1822, Iturbide was crowned Emperor
Agustín I. Those who were opposed to
having an emperor took up arms. The
next year General Antonio López de
Santa Anna dissolved the empire, and
Iturbide fled to Italy.

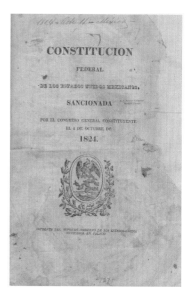

The 1824 Constitution

By October 1824, a constitution was written declaring the nation a republic called the United Mexican States. It would guide the young nation through many political upheavals, invasions, and rebellions.

In 1829, General Vicente Guerrero was chosen as president. By now Mexico included the territory of Texas and was the largest Spanish-speaking country in the world. President Guerrero expelled the Spanish, which resulted in their invading Mexico. When the Spanish army landed, so many men got sick with yellow fever that they surrendered and left.

During the first fifty years, there were fifty governments. In 1833, General Santa Anna was named president. Over the next twenty-two years, the presidency changed hands thirty-six times. Santa Anna served as president eleven of those times, until he was forced out of office in 1855.

General Santa Anna

The battle of the Alamo in San Antonio, Texas

The Wars

The Texas War began in 1836 when Texas—then part of Mexico—declared its independence. President Santa Anna overwhelmed the Texans at the Alamo. He then ordered that all the survivors be shot. The Texans went after Santa Anna and captured him. He signed a treaty that gave the republic of Texas the lands north of the Rio Grande.

By 1830, France had recognized the young nation of Mexico. Relations between the two countries were good, and many French lived in Mexico. But the Mexican government made them pay high taxes. When the French ambassador complained, he was expelled. In 1838, he returned with an army and demanded that Mexico compensate the French businessmen. One was a baker whose shop had been destroyed by Mexican soldiers, and so the conflict was called the Pastry War.

When the Mexicans refused to pay, the French bombarded Fort San Juan de Ulúa near Veracruz. Santa Anna rushed into battle. A cannon ball cut off his left leg below the knee, which he buried with full military honors. Santa Anna then signed a pact with the French, and Mexico paid the money.

The French army attacks a Mexican fort.

When the United States granted statehood to Texas, Mexico declared that this violated their treaty. President James Polk invaded Mexico, and Santa Anna sent troops across the border in 1846. This was the beginning of the Mexican-American War.

In September 1847, American forces landed in Veracruz and marched into Mexico City. Fifty cadets of the military college were left to defend the Chapultepec Castle. Rather than be taken prisoner, six of them wrapped themselves in the Mexican flag and leaped to their deaths on the rocks below. They are remembered today as *Los Niños Héroes*.

In February 1848, the defeated Santa Anna signed the Treaty of Guadalupe Hidalgo, which gave the United States not only the border territories between Texas and Mexico but also the land that is now Colorado, New Mexico, Nevada, Arizona, California, and parts of Utah and Wyoming. In exchange, Mexico was paid fifteen million dollars. By now, Mexico had lost half its land.

Though the United States gained a great deal of territory from the war, not everyone had been in favor of it. Abraham Lincoln, who was a congressman at the time, was against the war with Mexico and called it "the most unjust war there ever was."

The American army attacking Chapultepec Castle

Benito Juárez

By the mid-1850s, Mexico had two opposing political groups, the conservatives and the liberals. The conservatives wanted a return to church and military rule. The liberals wanted a democratic Mexico. The leader of the liberals was a Zapotec Indian named Benito Juárez. He had been orphaned as a child and served as a house boy. With the help of a patron he went on to study law. The controversy between the liberals and conservatives was called the War of the Reform.

In 1857, Juárez presented a new, democratic constitution, and in 1858, he was named president. The following year the conservatives took over Mexico City and had Juárez arrested. After his release he fled to Veracruz, where he set up a new government to oppose that of the conservatives in Mexico City. While in Veracruz he wrote the Laws of Reform, which separated the church from the state. These laws remain the foundation of the Mexican government today.

Both conservatives and liberals asked for help from other nations. Spain recognized the conservatives, while President Buchanan of the United States recognized the liberals. In

1861, the liberal army defeated the conservatives, and Juárez was elected president. That same year, Abraham Lincoln took office and also recognized the Juárez government. The men respected each other, since both had risen from humble origins.

"Respect for the rights of others brings peace."
—*Benito Juárez*

Emperor Maximilian

The conservatives asked France to help them return to an empire, and in December 1861, the French army invaded Veracruz. On May 5, 1862, the Mexicans under the command of Generals Ignacio Zaragoza and Porfirio Díaz defeated the French army at the Battle of Puebla de los Angeles. This victory is celebrated today as the *Cinco de Mayo* (Fifth of May).

This was only a temporary victory for Mexico. The next year, the French defeated the liberal army and entered Mexico City. Again, Juárez had to leave the capital. The conservatives and Napoleon III of France offered the crown to Ferdinand Maximilian of Habsburg, the Archduke of Austria. He arrived

A Mexican lancer fighting the French

Emperor Maximilian with his wife, Princess Carlota

in Mexico in 1864 with his wife, the beautiful Belgian Princess Carlota.

Once the American Civil War ended in 1865, the United States turned its attention to international affairs and insisted that the French leave Mexico. Napoleon recalled his troops and abandoned the emperor. Maximilian surrendered to the liberal army and was executed on June 19, 1867. Two days later General Porfirio Díaz led the army into Mexico City, and Benito Juárez was re-elected president for a third term.

The young general Porfirio Díaz

President Porfirio Díaz

The Porfiriato

For the next ten years, with the support of the United States, Benito Juárez served as liberal president. When Juárez died in 1872, General Porfirio Díaz took over. His reign is referred to as the Porfiriato. Díaz ruled for the next thirty-three years by rewriting the constitution and holding fake elections. During the Porfiriato the economy grew strong, but most

The Palacio de Bellas Artes museum and theater built during the Porfiriato

wealth lay in the hands of foreigners. Only a few Mexicans lived well; the majority were terribly poor.

The Indians and the *mestizos* rebelled because their lands were being taken away by large landowners. Díaz used an army of rural police called the *rurales* to protect the landowners. As more industries were built, many *campesinos*, or farm workers, went to find jobs in foreign-owned factories.

Cavalry soldiers suppressing protestors

By 1906, workers wanted fair wages and went out on strike. Díaz sent the army to stop the strikes by killing the workers. When newspapers criticized the government, editors and reporters were arrested. So few people could read at the time that newspapers used carved woodcuts to illustrate their stories.

Revolution

By the beginning of the twentieth century, workers and peasants were joining together to demand better working conditions. In 1910, Francisco I. Madero campaigned against Díaz as the candidate of the Anti-Reelection Party. He was arrested and jailed during the elections, so the eighty-year-old Porfirio Díaz won again. Following the election, Madero was released on bail. He was supposed to stay in Mexico, but instead he fled to San Antonio, Texas, where he called for a revolution. All over Mexico, men left their homes at night to join rebel groups gathering in the mountains and valleys. The armies of horsemen were growing.

Francisco Madero campaigning for the presidency

General Francisco (Pancho) Villa leading his revolutionary army

An Indian bandit known as Pancho Villa organized an army, joined Madero, and fought in the north. Another Indian, Emiliano Zapata, gathered an army of horsemen and laborers, called peons (landless farmers), and fought in the south. By 1910 only two percent of farmers owned their land. He wanted the land returned to the *campesinos* from the big landowners and corrupt government officials who had taken it.

General Emiliano Zapata

Not only did men fight but women, called *soldaderas*, and children went with them into battle. The railroads that connected the nation were a weapon for both the federal army and the revolutionaries. Horses traveled in the boxcars while men, women, and children rode on top.

On May 10, 1911, Ciudad Juárez, the city across the border from El Paso, Texas, fell to the revolutionaries, and Madero was named president.

A soldadera with her children

A boy soldier

After over thirty years in power, Porfirio Díaz was forced to resign and went into exile in Europe. Madero, the leader of the revolution, rode into Mexico City.

Fifteen-year-old Macedonio Manzano fought with the revolutionary army. In 1915 he was captured and executed.

Victoriano Huerta

Venustiano Carranza

President Madero asked the revolutionaries to lay down their arms. At first Zapata refused, but Madero convinced him. That's when the general of the government forces, Victoriano Huerta, ambushed Zapata's defenseless army. Zapata escaped but lost many of his men. Then Huerta had Madero murdered. In 1913, Huerta became the dictator of Mexico.

Venustiano Carranza, the governor of Coahuila, organized an army to fight Huerta. Álvaro Obregón and Pancho Villa led the rebellion in the north. Emiliano Zapata fought around Mexico City. Their battle cry was "Death to Huerta, down with the foreigners, Mexico for the Mexicans." The United States would not recognize Huerta's government because he had taken power illegally. Instead the United States sided with Carranza. To keep arms from reaching Huerta, President Woodrow Wilson sent the U. S. Navy to invade Veracruz in 1914. The town was defended by Pro Huerta naval cadets and citizens. Hundreds were killed. Later that year Carranza's army occupied Mexico

American sailors shooting at defenders of Veracruz

General "Black Jack" Pershing searching for Pancho Villa

City. Huerta was forced to resign and fled the country.

The U.S. Navy left an arsenal of arms, which Carranza used against Zapata and Villa. Pancho Villa, in a fury, raided Columbus, New Mexico, killing eighteen Americans and stealing horses. U.S. General "Black Jack" Pershing led the cavalry which included African American Buffalo soldiers into Mexico to capture Villa, but they never found him. Zapata was lured into an ambush in 1919 and killed by Carranza's soldiers. Even today, some people say that he is alive and has been seen in the mountains riding alone.

A mural by Diego Rivera in the National Palace

Fruits of the Revolution

A new Constitution was signed in 1917 that restored the traditional *ejido* system by which land was held in common in Indian villages. As the new president, Carranza's goal was to bring peace to the nation. But in the cities, workers were striking for better pay and conditions. In the countryside, *campesinos* were taking over the lands of big haciendas. The following year, General Álvaro Obregón overthrew Carranza. Pancho Villa was given a hacienda where he was later killed.

When Obregón was elected in 1920, he made sure that small towns had *ejidos*, on which farmers either worked their own plots or shared fields with other farmers. He also built schools and brought education to rural Indians.

The government sponsored great artists to paint murals on the walls of public

General Álvaro Obregón

36

buildings, showing the history of Mexico. Diego Rivera, José Clemente Orozco, David Siqueiros, and others painted the agonies and victories of the Mexican people.

General Plutarco Elías Calles was elected in 1924. He formed the National Revolutionary Party, which eventually became the Institutional Revolutionary Party (PRI). The PRI remained the dominant political party through the rest of the twentieth century.

Cristero soldiers defending a church

Relations between the revolutionary government and the church were very bad. Churches, schools, and hospitals were closed. Priests were killed, imprisoned, or deported. This brought about a bloody, armed conflict between 1926 and 1929 called the Cristero Rebellion. Obregón was re-elected in 1928 but was assassinated by a fanatic Catholic while celebrating his victory.

In 1934, Lázaro Cárdenas who fought in Madero's army when he was eighteen, became president. He distributed millions of acres of land to communities of landless peasants and nationalized railroads. In 1938, when the foreign oil companies refused to give workers a raise, Cárdenas took over the companies. These reforms made Cárdenas very popular with the Mexican people.

Crowds cheering the decision to nationalize the oil industry

A World War II poster

When German submarines torpedoed two Mexican ships, Mexico entered World War II as an ally of the United States in May 1942. Two hundred thousand Mexican hired hand workers (*braceros*) were invited to come north to replace the Americans who had gone to war. About one thousand Mexican citizens served in the United States' armed forces. One Mexican air squadron fought in the Philippines. Mexico supplied vital materials to the Allied war effort. Mexico prospered from its wartime activity and was able to put money into its universities and technical institutes.

Mexican braceros *working on American farms*

During the 1940s and 1950s, Mexico's economy continued to grow. In the 1960s, however, the economy grew worse because of inflation and population growth, which brought protesters into the streets. The gap between the rich and the very poor was widening. On October 2, 1968, 10,000 students gathered in Tlatelolco Plaza in Mexico City to demonstrate against the corrupt political system. Police and soldiers opened fire and killed 325 or more unarmed students. Five hundred were wounded and 2,000 arrested. These repressions created armed guerrilla groups both in the cities and the rural areas of Mexico, which continue to exist today.

The police beating demonstrators in Tlatelolco Plaza

A puppet figure of ex-president Salinas is hung in a plaza.

In 1993, President Carlos Salinas de Gortari signed the North American Free Trade Agreement (NAFTA) which dropped tariffs, or taxes on goods, among Mexico, Canada, and the United States. He also sold government banks, airlines, public utilities, and other services to private interests. After his term of office, Salinas fled the country to avoid testifying against his brother Raúl, who was involved in the murder of a high ranking PRI official. Many Mexicans blame Salinas for their economic problems.

Subcomandante Marcos

A New Century

On January 1, 1994, the Zapatista National Liberation Army (EZLN) in the southern state of Chiapas occupied four towns for four days and then retreated into the highland forests. They felt that by joining NAFTA, the rights of Mexico's *campesinos* and Indians were ignored in the name of profits. The leader of the Zapatistas is a former university lecturer called Subcomandante Marcos. He always wears a ski mask to hide his true identity. What they ask for is democracy, freedom, and justice for all Mexicans.

  The twentieth century began with a bloody revolution for

democracy and justice. Then the revolution became an institution that in time ignored the voices of the people. Politicians worked to save this institution from change. But change has come with the election of a candidate from a party other than the PRI.

Vicente Fox Quesada, candidate of the Partido de Acción Nacional (PAN) was elected in the year 2000. Most Mexicans, fed up with the PRI, voted for a non-PRI candidate for the first time in seventy-one years.

As Mexico enters a new millennium, the people cautiously look to see which road this president will take. Hopefully, he will take the Mexican people where they want to go.

President Vicente Fox Quesada

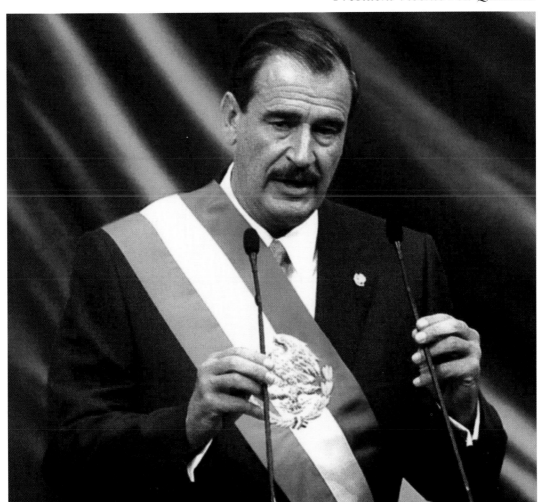

Timeline

7000 B.C. Nomadic tribes begin to grow corn and form communities

1500 B.C.–900 B.C. Olmec Civilization thrives along Gulf Coast

200 B.C. Unknown people build Teotihuacán

A.D. 200–900 Teotihuacán, Maya, and Zapotec civilizations

900–1200 The Toltec Empire controls the Valley of Mexico

1325 The Aztecs build Tenochtitlán

1420–1500 Aztecs rule over central and southern Mexico

1521 Hernán Cortés conquers the Aztec Empire

1810 Father Hidalgo begins the struggle for Mexican independence

1821 Mexico wins independence

1822 Iturbide is named Emperor Agustín I

1824 A new constitution proclaims Mexico a republic

1846–1848 Mexican-American War. United States defeats Mexico

1848 The Treaty of Guadalupe Hidalgo cedes one third of Mexico to the United States

1855 Period of reform by liberal government under Benito Juárez

1863 French troops occupy Mexico City

1864 Maximilian of Austria becomes emperor of Mexico

1867 Liberal forces led by Benito Juárez regain power

1867–1880, 1884–1911 Porfirio Díaz rules Mexico

1910–1911 Francisco Madero leads a revolution to overthrow Díaz

1913 Madero is murdered by General Huerta and becomes dictator

1914 United States forces occupy Veracruz; Huerta flees

1916 Pancho Villa invades New Mexico.

1917 Revolutionary Constitution is adopted

1919 President Carranza orders the assassination of Emiliano Zapata

1920 Carranza is assassinated; President Obregón begins social and economic reforms

1923 Francisco (Pancho) Villa is assassinated

1926 Catholics react to government oppression with the Cristero Rebellion

1929 National Revolutionary Party is formed

1934 Government under Lázaro Cárdenas distributes land to farmers

1938 Government takes over foreign oil company properties

1993 North American Free Trade Agreement (NAFTA) is signed

1994 Uprising by the native people in Chiapas

2000 Vicente Fox Quesada is elected president

Glossary

Words in *italics* are Spanish words in this book.

campesino: a rural day worker

codices: plural for codex, an ancient book

conquistador: Spanish for conqueror; plural, *conquistadores*

criollo: Spanish person born in New Spain

Cuauhtémoc: last leader of the Aztecs

ejido: land owned and worked by a community

emperor: ruler of an empire

empire: group of people or nations ruled by one person

grito: shout or cry

liberal: wanting change and reform

Mesoamerica: area between North and South America

mestizo: person born of Indian and Spanish parents

mulato: person born of African and Spanish parents

Nahuatl: Aztec language

Quetzalcoatl: ancient god and king of the Toltecs

republic: government chosen by its citizens

Tenochtitlán: capital city of the Aztecs

viceroy: vice-king, governor for the king

Find Out More

Ancona, George. *Mayeros: A Yucatec Maya Family*. New York: Lothrop, Lee & Shepard Books, 1997.

Irizarry, Carmen. *Passport to Mexico*. New York: Franklin Watts, 1987.

Kent, Deborah. *Mexico: Rich in Spirit and Tradition*. New York: Marshall Cavendish, 1996.

Photo Credits

All photographs by George Ancona except the following: title page, wood engraving of Zapata by José Guadalupe Posada; 2–3, map art by Rodica Prato; 4, lithograph by Carl Nebel; 5, Aztec gods from *Art Resource*; 6–7, mural of Tenochtitlán by Miguel Covarubias; 10, mural detail by Desiderio H. Xochitiotzin; 12, procession of the viceroy from Laurie Platt Winfrey, viceroy from *Art Resource*; 14, mural detail by José Clemente Orozco, portrait of José Maria Morelos from Laurie Platt Winfrey, mural detail by Juan O'Gorman from *Art Resource*; 17, anonymous painting of Iturbide entering Mexico City from Laurie Platt Winfrey; 18, coronation of Agustín I from Laurie Platt Winfrey, constitution from *Corbis*; 19, General Santa Anna from *Corbis*; 20, Battle of the Alamo from State Preservation Board of Texas; woodcut of French attacking fort by José Guadalupe Posada, American army attacking Chapultepec Castle from *Corbis*; 27, Maximilian and Carlota from *Corbis*/Hulton Deutche Collection, Porfirio Díaz from Fototeca-INAH; 28, President Porfiro Díaz from *Corbis*; 29, woodcut by José Guadalupe Posada; 30, Madero campaigning from Museo de Intervenciones; 31, Pancho Villa by Agustín Casasola from *Corbis*/Hulton Deutche Collection, Zapata by Agustín Casasola from Fototeca-INAH; 32, Soldadera by Agustín Casasola; 33, boy soldier by Agustín Casasola from Fototeca-INAH, boy soldier from John O. vb Hardman Collection; 34, President Huerta by Agustín Casasola from Fototeca-INAH, sailors firing machine gun from *Corbis*; 35, General Pershing from *Bettmann*; 36, Alvaro Obregón from *Corbis*; 38, soldiers on church roof from *Bettmann*; 39, demonstration from *Bettmann*; 40 World War II poster from Margolies and Moss; 41, braceros by Carlos Marentes from *AP/Wide World Photos*; 42, soldiers beating protestor from *AP/Wide World Photos*; 44, Subcomandante Marcos, *AP/Wide World Photos*; 45, President Fox, AFP.

Index

Page numbers in **boldface** are illustrations.

Photo © Mary Morris

About the Author

While writing this book, George Ancona discovered the sources of his own history. The songs his parents sang and the stories they told him as he grew up in Brooklyn, New York, were the beginning. Now he understands the conditions that brought his parents to this country from Mexico in the early 1900s. He now lives in New Mexico, a part of old Mexico.